EXPLORING THE
AMERICAN WEST

EXPLORING THE
AMERICAN WEST
JAMES L. COLLINS

Franklin Watts
New York/London/Toronto/Sydney
A First Book/1989

Photographs courtesy of:
The Granger Collection: pp. 10 (both), 11, 18, 21, 23,
27 (both), 30, 35, 39, 48, 51 (bottom), 53, 56; Glens
Falls Insurance Company: p. 14; New York Public
Library Picture Collection: pp. 16, 20, 26, 55; The
Bettmann Archive: pp. 17, 33, 51 (top); Indepen-
dence Hall Collection: p. 24; South Dakota State
College: p. 36; Joslyn Art Museum, Omaha, Ne-
braska: 43; Library of Congress: 59.

Library of Congress Cataloging-in-Publication Data

Collins, James L., 1945-

Exploring the American West / by James L. Collins.
p.   cm. — (A First book)
Bibliography: p.
Includes index.
Summary: Recounts the exploits of explorers of the
American West, from Daniel Boone in the late 1700s
to John Charles Frémont in the 1850s,
ISBN 0-531-10684-5
1. West (U.S.) — Discovery and exploration — Juvenile literture.
2. West (U.S.) — Description and travel — To 1848 — Juvenile
literature.   3. West (U.S.) — Description and travel — 1848-1860 —
Juvenile literature.   4. Explorers — West (U.S.) — History — Juvenile
literature.   5. United States — Exploring expeditions — Juvenile
literature.   [1. Explorers.   2. West (U.S.) — Discovery and
exploration.   3. United States — Exploring expeditions.]
I. Title.   II. Series.
F591.C735   1989
978 .01 — dc19   88-30337 CIP AC

CONTENTS

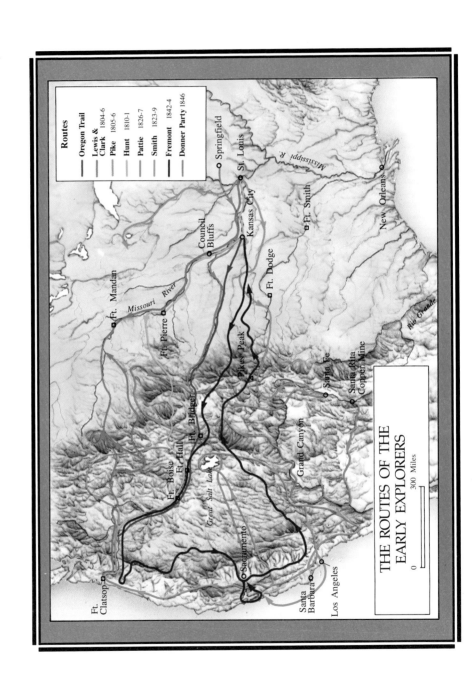

THE ROUTES OF THE EARLY EXPLORERS

0   300 Miles

Routes

Oregon Trail
Lewis & Clark 1804-6
Pike 1805-6
Hunt 1810-1
Pattie 1826-7
Smith 1823-9
Fremont 1842-4
Donner Party 1846

Springfield
St. Louis
Mississippi R.
Council Bluffs
Kansas City
Ft. Smith
New Orleans
Ft. Dodge
Ft. Mandan
Missouri River
Ft. Pierre
Pikes Peak
Santa Fe
Santa Rita Copper Mine
Rio Grande
Ft. Bridger
Grand Canyon
Ft. Hall
Ft. Boise
Great Salt Lake
Sacramento
Ft. Clatsop
Santa Barbara
Los Angeles

INTRODUCTION

Americans have always been a curious people. And ever since the Pilgrims landed at Plymouth Rock in 1620, we have been moving westward. It is the legendary frontierspeople who intrigue us and whom we remember best. But how did these people live? How did they survive in a land whose western borders were so dark and mysterious they could only be called "the wilderness?"

They cleared the wilderness land, burned brush, and planted corn and wheat among the stumps. They built crude cabins of hickory, walnut, or persimmon logs, laid a wooden floor, and made windowpanes of paper soaked in lard or bear grease.

The men wore homemade hunting shirts and deerskin leggings, the women plain dresses; fabric was homespun—woven of fibers made on the spinning wheel by the hearth. They pegged their chairs

Above: *a typical log cabin on the American frontier.* Right: *the early pioneers wore handmade clothing.*

and tables together from wooden slabs; they ground their meal in homemade block mortars; they ate with tin spoons from pine serving plates; they went barefoot or wore skin moccasins. Their food was hog-and-hominy grits, with roast venison, wild turkeys or partridges, and fish from the nearest stream. For defense against Indians, the scattered settlers built a fort at some central spring, with bulletproof blockhouses and stockade.

The country they lived in stretched from the ragged forest clearings of the Mohawk Valley down the eastern fringes of the Alleghenies, on through

Pioneers hunted, fished, and cleared the land for farming. They were a hardy group of people.

the Shenandoah Valley in Virginia, and into the Piedmont area of the Carolinas. It was a part of the country that brought forth sturdy pioneer farmers who would steadily widen the belt of settlement and civilization. The further west they moved, the more resourceful these men and women became, for if nothing else, it was the way of the land.

This book will cover approximately one hundred years, from the exploits of Daniel Boone after the French and Indian War of 1754–1763, to the expeditions of John Charles Frémont in the 1840s and 1850s. The men described here were not the only explorers to make their way through the American West. Nearly all of them had a counterpart, another person who lived in their lifetime, who explored the same land they did. The only difference is that the explorers you are about to read of have been given more credit than the others. They are generally acknowledged to have made more significant contributions to the exploration of the American West.

DANIEL BOONE
OPENING UP KENTUCKY

If ever a man became a legend in his own time, it was Daniel Boone. Before his death in 1820, he was known throughout the country as a famous hunter, explorer, and Indian fighter.

Born on November 2, 1734, near Reading, Pennsylvania, Boone received little schooling as a youngster. But if his grammar and spelling weren't the best, young Daniel felt right at home in the woods and quickly learned how to "read sign," the fine art of being able to spot and track quarry in the wilderness. This part of his knowledge was taught to him by friendly Indians and is probably responsible for the deep understanding and appreciation he had for the Indian throughout his life.

Boone is generally credited with the discovery of Kentucky, but a good many adventurers had entered the "Dark and Bloody Ground" (as Kentucky was known) nearly two decades before

The French and Indian War. This is the battle of Rogers' Rock, fought by Major Robert Rogers' Rangers near Lake George, New York.

Boone. The French and Indian War activity (1754–1763) temporarily interrupted further exploration. Boone served as a wagonmaster for General Braddock in the disastrous Battle of the Wilderness in 1755.

Talk of the exploits of other men exploring Kentucky made Boone restless. The Cumberland Gap had been discovered by hunters, the bluegrass country by the traders who followed. What was needed was someone who could put it all together by finding a route from the southern back country that would enable others to enter this newfound paradise. Daniel Boone set out with determination to blaze that trail.

Boone's first try exploring Kentucky in 1767 was a failure. The country he entered looked nothing like the description he had been given. The second try, in the winter of 1767–68, was just as bad. He spent several months alone, roaming in the wilderness and dodging Indian war parties, as he lived off the country and slept where he could find shelter. His wanderings took him as far north as the Ohio River, but he still failed to find the route he was searching for. On his third trip, in the summer of 1771, after having been resupplied, he and the handful of men with him were nearly killed near Cumberland Gap when warring Indians took their horses, furs, and supplies.

Once word of Boone's ill fortune was spread around, a group of hunters decided to band together and roam the same country Boone had in the fall of 1770. They were so successful that they did so again the following year, hunting, trapping, and exploring the land. But once these explorers had come and gone, it was the land speculators who set their caps on conquering the wilds of "Kaintuck."

Daniel Boone, one of America's most famous hunters and explorers. Facing page: *Boone coming through the Cumberland Gap.*

There was a fortune to be made in selling such land to would-be settlers, but a trail that would offer safe passage had yet to be found. So far the only trails that had been used by those entering this land were those made by the Indians who inhabited the land and by animals.

A Judge Richard Henderson was able to work out a contract of sorts with the Cherokee Indians in 1775. While his negotiations with the Indians were still in progress, the confident Henderson sent Boone with thirty axmen to cut a road to the Kentucky River, where he planned to build his first settlement. It was the beginning of what would become known as the Wilderness Road. Boone and his men began on Holston River and worked their way westward. In ten days, they were joined by Henderson himself, who had brought along some forty riflemen to protect Boone's party. He also brought a number of Negro slaves and a small wagon train with pack horses loaded with provisions and ammunition.

At the Cumberland Gap, the group met forty pioneers in retreat to the east, scared to death over news of an Indian uprising. But that didn't deter

Henderson, who was now more determined than ever to reach his goal. And that he did. Along the way, some who had come with him thus far struck out on their own trail further west to what would become known as Harrodsburg.

Once they had reached the Kentucky River, Boone and his men began staking claims of their own to the surrounding land they would settle on. It was the beginning of Boonesborough, a fortlike structure which, along with Harrodsburg, became

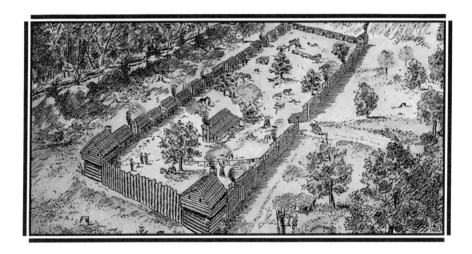

Fort Boonesborough, Kentucky.
The fort established by
Boone and his men in 1778.

one of the first footholds in the wilderness called "Kaintuck." It wasn't entirely completed until after the start of the American Revolution.

It wasn't much later (1779) that a number of the Indian tribes would unite to try to force the white man from their land, just as the pioneers were trying to force the Indians out. It was Daniel Boone's heroism as an Indian fighter during those years that would make him a legend in our early frontier history.

But as an explorer, his probing of that "Dark and Bloody Ground" and the opening of the Wilderness Trail would forever remain his greatest feat. For, when they neared Boonesborough, the sight of tossing white clover, level bluegrass, and the gently flowing Kentucky River was to cheer many a weary traveler at the end of the Wilderness Road for decades to come.

After the American Revolution (1775–1783), our political leaders formed the Constitution our land would be ruled by, and the farmers of our volunteer army went back to working the land they loved and had fought for.

Thomas Jefferson, both a signer of the Declaration of Independence and a president of the United States, had that same love of the land. A Virginia

With the opening of the Wilderness Trail (marked in red here), America's era of western expansion began.

landowner himself, Jefferson had a firm belief that the farmer and the plantation owner would be the corps of greatness of our country for years to come. As the third president of the United States (1801–1809), Jefferson purchased the Louisiana Territory from Napoleonic France in 1803. At the cost of $15 million, Jefferson more than doubled the size of our country.

Thomas Jefferson immediately began to plan a probe of this newly purchased land to find out exactly what it was he had bought sight unseen. That probe became known as the Lewis and Clark Expedition.

It was Thomas Jefferson, as the third president of the United States, who purchased more than 800,000 square miles of territory from France. This was the Louisiana Purchase.

LEWIS AND CLARK
THE VOYAGE OF EXPLORATION

Perhaps the most famous of all expeditions, the Lewis and Clark Expedition took place one year after President Jefferson made the Louisiana Purchase in 1803. That expedition has been called "incomparably the most perfect achievement of its kind in the history of the world." It was as important to opening up the lands west of the Mississippi River as Daniel Boone's opening of the Wilderness Trail had been to those searching for a way west through the Appalachian Mountains. And if the words "Dark and Bloody Land" struck fear into the hearts of those who ventured into Kentucky, it was the sheer vastness of the Louisiana Territory that most held Lewis and Clark in awe.

The purpose of the expedition was twofold. Jefferson wanted not only to explore the scientific possibilities of this new land, but also to open up the Missouri River as a trade route between Indian and

American traders. Up until that time, most of the fur trading in the far west had been done between the Indians and the French or British. By opening up the Missouri River, Jefferson thought the Indians he so admired would find it easier to travel downstream toward the Mississippi and trade with the Americans. To lead such an expedition, Jefferson needed a trustworthy, dependable person. He didn't have far to look to find the man he wanted.

Meriwether Lewis (1774–1809) was a native Virginian and a neighbor of Jefferson's. He was as enthusiastic about science and the exploration of this new land as the president himself.

Meriwether Lewis, chosen by President Jefferson to lead an expedition into the Louisiana Territory.

As his second-in-command, Lewis chose William Clark (1770–1838), a friend from the army and younger brother of George Rogers Clark, a hero of the American Revolution in the West. The two men couldn't have been more different. Lewis, an experienced woodsman and soldier in his own right, tended to keep to himself. Clark, on the other hand, was an outgoing man, almost a born diplomat, and an even more experienced woodsman than Lewis. But despite their differences, the two men worked well together.

Lewis chose William Clark as his second-in-command on his journeys.

Lewis and Clark spent several months training the group of men they would call their "Corps of Discovery" for life in the wilderness. On May 14, 1804, the expedition left an area near St. Louis on a twenty-eight-month journey. Lewis and Clark and their men would be forced to endure months of cold, weeks of hunger and fatigue, days of backbreaking labor under the prairie's sweltering sun, and occasional harassment from the Indians. Yet they maintained near-perfect discipline of the twenty-seven-man party throughout the entire expedition, losing only one man, who most likely died of appendicitis.

The group covered about two thousand miles on the outward trip in eighteen months, carefully mapping and describing the country. They also laid a basis for American competition with the rich British fur-trading companies, such as the Hudson's Bay Company. Geographically, their trek into the wilderness greatly enlarged our knowledge of what we now call continental America. When they had returned from the headwaters of the Columbia and Missouri rivers, Lewis and Clark had gained a whole new knowledge of what this virgin land was like. Their reports contained descriptions of animals as large as a grizzly bear and as small as a

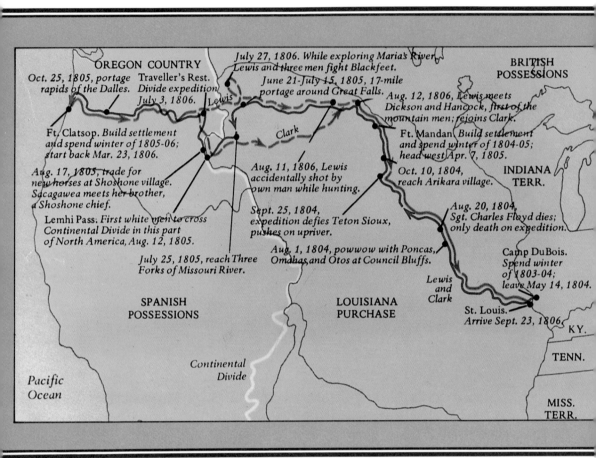

OREGON COUNTRY

Oct. 25, 1805, portage Traveller's Rest.
rapids of the Dalles. Divide expedition
July 3, 1806. Lewis

July 27, 1806. While exploring Maria's River,
Lewis and three men fight Blackfeet.
June 21-July 15, 1805, 17-mile
portage around Great Falls.

BRITISH
POSSESSIONS

Aug. 12, 1806, Lewis meets
Dickson and Hancock, first of the
mountain men; rejoins Clark.

Clark

Ft. Clatsop. Build settlement
and spend winter of 1805-06;
start back Mar. 23, 1806.

Ft. Mandan. Build settlement
and spend winter of 1804-05;
head west Apr. 7, 1805.

INDIANA
TERR.

Aug. 17, 1805, trade for
new horses at Shoshone village.
Sacagawea meets her brother,
a Shoshone chief.

Aug. 11, 1806, Lewis
accidentally shot by
own man while hunting.

Oct. 10, 1804,
reach Arikara village.

Lemhi Pass: First white men to cross
Continental Divide in this part
of North America, Aug. 12, 1805.

Sept. 25, 1804,
expedition defies Teton Sioux,
pushes on upriver.

Aug. 20, 1804,
Sgt. Charles Floyd dies;
only death on expedition.

Aug. 1, 1804, powwow with Poncas,
Omahas, and Otos at Council Bluffs.

Camp DuBois.
Spend winter
of 1803-04;
leave May 14, 1804.

July 25, 1805, reach Three
Forks of Missouri River.

Lewis
and
Clark

St. Louis.
Arrive Sept. 23, 1806.

KY.

SPANISH
POSSESSIONS

LOUISIANA
PURCHASE

Continental
Divide

TENN.

Pacific
Ocean

MISS.
TERR.

Above: *a map showing the route Lewis and Clark
took from St. Louis to the Oregon Country.
Top right: members of the Lewis and Clark expedition building a line of huts. Bottom right:
shooting bears during the expedition.*

mosquito, and plants and animals that had never before been imaginable to the human eye. Unfortunately, even with the publication of their reports in 1814, the first complete critical edition of their work was not done until 1893, long after both men had died.

Two men who seemed so different worked side by side on a journey that was not only the pinnacle of their careers, but a turning point in the history of this nation. The "Corps of Discovery" led a Voyage of Discovery that only in the last century has received the credit it so long deserved, but under a slightly different name.

Today we call it the Lewis and Clark Expedition.

A number of exploring parties would venture into the Louisiana Purchase during the fifty-year period following the return of Lewis and Clark. These new explorers would blaze new trails for others to follow as they headed west. One of their discoveries was so important and so big that it had to be discovered from both the east and the west. But then, finding a path through the Rocky Mountains was a big task.

ROBERT STUART AND JED SMITH
DISCOVERING THE SOUTH PASS

The discovery of the South Pass in the Rocky Mountains did a great deal to open up the West for travelers headed for Oregon and California. Yet this pass was so big that it took two men to discover it, Robert Stuart (1785–1848) from the west side in 1812, and Jed Smith (1799–1831) from the east side in 1824.

By 1810 Robert Stuart had gone to Montreal, Canada, where he soon joined John Jacob Astor's Pacific Fur Company. Astor, one of the great names in the history of the fur trade, was then planning two separate expeditions to the mouth of the Columbia River, where Lewis and Clark had sighted the Pacific Ocean. One expedition would be by ship around the southern tip of Cape Horn. This was the only feasible way to get from the east coast to the west by sea. The other journey would be by land to

*The discovery of the South Pass
in the Rocky Mountains
helped open up new routes for
travelers heading West.*

the same destination. Stuart booked passage on the *Tonquin*, a ship with the Columbia expedition, and arrived at the new colony, Astoria, six months later, in March 1811. He proved to be a worthy man and, in the summer of 1812, was chosen by the partners to be the courier who would carry dispatches overland to Astor back east.

By no means did Stuart fashion himself to be a trailblazer, but before his trip was over, that was what he would become. It must be remembered that Stuart had never seen the land he would traverse, although members of the original expedition had come upon the Snake and Columbia rivers on the way west. In late June 1812, Stuart set out with only six men in his party to carry out his mission.

The journey was filled with danger as the men ventured into parts of the West that had never before been seen by white men. After following the Columbia River and part of the Snake, Stuart came upon some friendly Indians. One of them informed him that an easier route through the massive Rocky Mountains lay to the south. The Indian agreed to act as a guide in exchange for gifts that ranged from powder and ball to blankets and trinkets. The little band of men traveled twenty-five miles to the south before coming upon the western entrance to what would become known as the South Pass.

Although its name suggests a dramatic gap in the Rocky Mountain barrier, South Pass is actually a saddle between the southern extremes of the Wind River Range and the Antelope Hills to the south. Far from appearing distinctive, it is a broad, high plain, twenty miles wide, which rises from the Wyoming Basin to a height of 7,550 feet above sea level. To the east of it lay a portion of the Sweetwater River and a narrow canyon, dominated by three-hundred-foot cliffs. These would later be known as Devil's Gate.

It was October 1812 when Stuart and his weary band of men made their way through this newly found pass. The trail they had forged from Astoria to South Pass had been the hardest part of the journey, but it still wasn't until the spring of 1813 that they reached St. Louis. From there Stuart went to New York to deliver his dispatches to Astor.

Robert Stuart's "discovery" of the South Pass is seldom noted with the awe and attention that Daniel Boone's Wilderness Road or the Lewis and Clark Expedition receives. But if the Lewis and Clark Expedition did for the frontier what Boone's Wilderness Trail had done for those pioneers yearning to move west in the colonial days, Stuart's find was that much more important. Between 1841 and 1853, the South Pass was used by 150,000 persons on

Riding between rocky cliffs

their way west, among them Mormon settlers of Utah and the California gold seekers of 1849. Even more famous was the trail Stuart and his men had blazed from Astoria to South Pass. It became the most widely used trail in the country for the longest period of time. In the two decades that followed, an exodus of settlers looking for prime farmland made their way to this country.

Twelve years after Stuart's discovery in 1812, South Pass was discovered from the east side by Jed Smith.

Smith was tall and lean, for the work of a mountain man in those early years of the trade in the 1820s would take a few pounds off even the stoutest of men. He also carried a butcher's knife in his belt and a Bible in his bedroll. An odd combination perhaps, but an effective one for young Smith.

Smith joined the Ashley expedition with the intent "of becoming a first-rate hunter, of making myself thoroughly acquainted with the Indians, of tracing out the sources of the Columbia River, and of making the whole profitable to me."

In the fall of 1823, Smith and eleven others left the Ashley party on the Upper Missouri River, intent on crossing what we now call the Badlands of the Dakotas. Through trade with the Sioux, the

*Emigrants to the West pass
a rural schoolhouse.*

*While no true picture of Jed Smith
exists, artist Harvey Dunn has
succeeded in capturing the spirit of
this famous explorer and trapper.*

group hoped to obtain more horses for the expedition. It was felt that they might meet a Captain Weber in the Yellowstone area and join forces with his group for the spring hunt. It was also on this trek that Jedediah Strong Smith was to gain a reputation as a strong, tough, and courageous leader.

Near the Wind River, Smith and his men were walking their mounts over the brushy bottom land when they were surprised by a grizzly bear. Smith and the huge bear met face to face, and the bear mauled him. However, in a little more than a week, Smith was up and about again, healing fast from his wounds. He and his men scouted the area as much as possible, then wintered a while with the Crow, whose territory they had entered. Although the terrain was his primary interest, Smith did receive information from the Crow that an excellent area to trap beaver could be found on the far side of the Wind River Mountains. They said that one only needed to walk along the banks of the river and club the beaver rather than trap them.

At first this must have sounded outrageous, but the land was so plentiful that it might have been the truth too. With that in mind, Smith obtained directions on how to reach the western slope of the mountains and, in February 1824, he found himself exploring the Devil's Gate and the twenty-mile-wide expanse that would be known thereafter as South Pass.

Unfortunately, Smith never made it the entire way through South Pass to the western slope, for it was still winter and the snow made it impossible for man or beast. Taking shelter in Sweetwater Valley, the group of men waited impatiently for the weather to ease up. Finally, during the second week of March, with game scarce and the compulsion for the spring hunt upon them all, Smith and his men made their way up the Sweetwater River once more. Spring had yet to arrive, however, and this time the group met with gale force winds, which slowed them down considerably. But one week after they'd started, feeling as cold and miserable as humanly possible, Smith and his men made camp, having finally crossed South Pass.

During the 1840s covered wagons began moving west with men, women, and children who were looking for a new life in Oregon. To travel from St. Louis to the mouth of the Columbia River took several months. To follow the path blazed by Lewis and Clark, up the Missouri River to its northernmost branch in present day Montana, would be disastrous, for the wagon train would never reach

*Evening camp for
pioneers traveling West*

its destination before a harsh winter set in. By using the South Pass to go *through* the Rocky Mountains, rather than follow Lewis and Clark's trail *over* them, those pioneers were able to cut several hundred miles off the distance they had to travel to their destination.

The fur trade and the discovery of the South Pass, combined with William Becknell's blazing of the Sante Fe Trail, are generally considered to be the three most important events to add to the opening of the West in the 1820s.

When the mountain man invaded the Rocky Mountains, there were a number of rediscoveries, not the least of which was the South Pass. But the mountain man didn't stop at exploring the Rocky Mountains. Once past the Rockies, several of these hearty men kept on moving west until only the Pacific Ocean stopped them. In fact, Jed Smith was one of the first white men to be greeted by the Spanish who had settled the land we now call the state of California. But he was by no means the last. Six years after Smith's visit, another mountain man made his way into California. The difference between these two explorations was that where Jed Smith had taken the southern route, across the Mojave Desert, this new visitor went via the northern route. One thing both of these mountain men had in common in venturing into this land was the desire to know more about the land and the people they would be dealing with.

That second explorer was a mountain man by the name of Joseph Reddeford Walker.

JOSEPH REDDEFORD WALKER
OPENING CALIFORNIA
WITH A BIT OF MYSTERY

Joe Walker (1798–1876) is best described as one of the most versatile of the early explorers.

Originally from Tennessee, Walker moved west to Missouri in 1818 where he raised stock before exploring the Mexican Southwest.

In 1832, Walker was hired by Benjamin Bonneville as field commander of a well-equipped party of 110 men he took west. Their purpose, or so Bonneville stated, was to trap and trade in the land. Since Bonneville was a failure at the fur trade, but nearly always had money to back his ventures, it seems likely that a bit of espionage may well have been involved in his mission. After all, the United States government was always interested in information concerning the lands held by the Mexican and British governments and could easily have financed such a mission.

Joseph Reddeford Walker, a man
whose passion in life was
exploring unknown regions.

Everything about Bonneville's venture seems controversial, but one thing is now certain. Although Walker did raise a force of forty volunteers to follow him from the 1833 rendezvous at Green River on to California, it wasn't a spur-of-the-moment thought. Bonneville had intended for Walker to enter California as early as January 1832. Making preparations for his mission, Bonneville visited the State Department in Washington and obtained a passport and visa from the Mexican consul in the mountain man's name. All of this would make Walker's entry into the territory of California legal.

In late July 1833, Walker and his men left, stopping four days later at Bear River, northwest of the Great Salt Lake. For nearly a week, Walker's men hunted and made jerky (meat that has been cut into long strips and dried in the sun), not stopping until each man in the party had a minimum of sixty pounds of jerky in his pack. Such preparation was unusual; most hunters in those days gorged themselves when there was plenty of food and starved when game was scarce. Walker's foresight made him quite different from his peers.

Joe Walker had a definite plan in mind and anticipated his needs. It was California he was headed for, and he made use of information learned through the exploits of others who had gone before him. Only three expeditions had previously made it to California, and two of those were by Jed Smith, in 1826 and 1827. (The third was made from the northwest in 1829 by Peter Skene Ogden.) Smith and his small party of fifteen men had set out in search of new areas in which to find beaver. Ill-prepared, they nearly died as they crossed the Mojave Desert of the southwest, twice crossing the same terrain. Walker and his men, on the other hand, carried enough supplies for one year, each man having several mounts.

With an additional twenty men picked up at Bear Lake, it may well have been the size of Walker's group that made their trek easier. But it is just as probable that it was Walker's own charm—and a few gifts—that got the Indians of that region to loosen their tongues and give the brigade leader the directions he needed.

Where Smith had taken the southern route across present-day Nevada, Walker struck a trail across the northern part of that state, following the Humboldt River to Humboldt Sink. It was while camping here that Walker soon found himself and his men surrounded by Paiute Indians who didn't look too friendly.

Walker told the chiefs he met that day that his

long rifle would kill any and all of them if they started a war. To prove his point, Walker shot several ducks sitting in nearby water, as did several of his men, greatly impressing the Paiutes.

Walker and his men then headed southwest over wild land. By the end of September, they were following the eastern slope of the Sierra Nevada range, looking for a pass that would take them to California on the western slope. By that time, they had also virtually exhausted their supply of jerked beef. Occasionally horses were slaughtered to feed the men. Still, the men forged on, heading west now, for they had found their entrance into the golden land of California in present-day Yosemite Valley. It took nearly a month to get through the mountains, fighting snow and icy trails, with the threat of avalanche always present.

On October 20, Walker and his men became perhaps the first whites to take in the sight of the Yosemite Valley. Horse and man had to be lowered into the valley by rope, a dangerous feat. When that was done, the men found game to feast on. With lifted spirits, they moved on, discovering a stand of the giant sequoia redwood trees, another first for whites in that time. But most important to Walker was the fact that he and his men had blazed a new trail through the Sierra Nevada into California.

Walker and his men headed for San Francisco, then turned south, moving along the coast to Monterey, where they wintered until mid-February 1834. The men moved south along the San Joaquin Valley, followed the Kern River eastward, and made their way through a narrow valley in the lower Sierras that is now called Walker Pass. They then headed north along the mountain range until they picked up the trail that led to the Humboldt River. By then it was June, and they had made it back to Ham's Fork of the Green River for the 1834 rendezvous. They had been gone one year.

Joe Walker's exploration of the Sierra Nevada and California was only the first of many in the career of a man whose passion in life seemed to be exploring unknown regions. As someone once described Walker: "He was one of the best leaders I have ever met, a good hunter and trapper, thoroughly versed in Indian signs and possessed of good knowledge of the mountains. He could find water quicker than any man I ever met."

In a land where water was the lifeline for all who traveled it, Joe Walker could hardly receive higher praise.

By the time the era of the mountain man began to fade in the early '40s, so many new discoveries had

*What it may have looked like when
the mountain men camped for the night.
Illustration by Frederic Remington.*

been made about the wilderness area west of the Mississippi River that the government decided to take a hand in the exploration business. In 1845 John L. O'Sullivan, editor of the *Democratic Review,* would coin the term "Manifest Destiny" in an editorial concerning the right of the United States government to annex the Republic of Texas. The phrase was soon broadened into what most Americans perceived as a God-given right to seize every bit of land between the Atlantic and Pacific oceans and make it part of the United States of America. This is just what we spent the next sixty years doing.

By 1845, the government had indeed taken an interest in finding new paths out west. A young officer who had begun his career as a second lieutenant in the U.S. Corps of Topographical Engineers was on his way to becoming a legend in his own time.

JOHN CHARLES FREMONT
HOW LEGENDS ARE MADE

For a man who later in his life was referred to as "the Great Pathfinder," John Charles Frémont (1813–1890) leaves much to be desired. A closer look at his "accomplishments" might well indicate that a more proper title for the man would be "the Great Promoter."

Handsome and intelligent, Frémont was the perfect image of a hero in an age when expansion in our country was taking place more than it was being talked about. When he fell in love with and secretly married Jessie Benton, daughter of the powerful Missouri senator, Thomas Hart Benton, in 1841, a career of fame and fortune must have seemed assured. But even if it weren't, Frémont could never have found a woman more supportive and devoted to him than Jessie.

There is a bit of mystery attached to Frémont's expeditions, which makes the legend built up

Explorer and Army officer John Charles Frémont

Jessie Benton, Frémont's wife, wrote up her husband's findings about the new lands he explored.

around him that much more interesting. Senator Benton felt strongly about westward expansion and was able to get his son-in-law appointed as the head of three expeditions between 1842 and 1845. As far as the public knew, Frémont was opening up new paths for them to take to Oregon and California. But the expeditions were actually secret missions that would shape the course of American policy.

The first secret mission was in 1842. As in subsequent expeditions, Frémont didn't break any new ground in his travels. Rather, he employed mountain men such as Kit Carson, who became a lifelong friend to Frémont, to lead him through routes already familiar to the experienced frontiersman. To travel along the Platte River, cross the South Pass, and explore the Wind River Range, as was done on his first trip, was nothing new. The fact that the high point of the expedition seems to have been that Frémont climbed a summit that he christened Frémont Peak makes the whole trip sound frivolous.

In fact, what Frémont reported to the Congress—detailed descriptions of the flora and fauna of the regions he traveled, as well as the location of water holes and Indian tribes—became an overnight best seller. It was Jessie Frémont who

*Frémont's exploring party at
Fort Laramie, Wyoming territory*

wrote up her husband's findings of this new land in as romantic a view as anyone could imagine. The original 10,000 copies that were printed were quickly snatched up by would-be settlers eager to be on their way to Oregon and California. Senator Benton himself could have done no better a job to promote westward expansion.

On Frémont's second expedition (1843–1844), again with Kit Carson as guide, he made a vain attempt to find a passage through the Central Rockies, explored the Great Salt Lake region, and arrived at Marcus Whitman's mission in the Oregon country in late fall. He then followed the Cascades down to what is now Nevada and foolishly tried to cross the Sierra Nevada range in midwinter, barely getting his men through alive. This journey alone could have assured Frémont immortality. His report, once again written by Jessie, expounded on the agricultural benefits of California, and described a large collection of scientific specimens and data that had been compiled. The report was well received and quickly sold out.

The purpose of Frémont's third expedition (1845), to survey the Arkansas and Red rivers, hardly seems worth mentioning, considering the outcome of it all. Frémont divided his party up. He took with him a hand-picked company of mountain

*Kit Carson was Frémont's guide
as well as lifelong friend.*

Frémont's third expedition in California

sharpshooters and blazed a trail through the Central Rockies and across the Great Basin to California. It is at this point in Frémont's life that controversy and the image of a stalwart, romantic hero who would do anything for his country emerge.

Like any expansionist, Frémont knew in his heart that California was destined to become a part of the American frontier. When war with Mexico seemed imminent in the spring of 1846, Frémont helped lead Americans in what has come to be known as the Bear Flag Revolt. His part in this insurgent movement is controversial at best. The controversy concerns a visit he received from Marine Lieutenant Archibald Gillespie just before the revolt began. For years historians have argued whether the Marine officer was or was not delivering a secret message from President James Polk. While Frémont rushed to establish a new government, the young Marine was conveniently killed in battle. When Stephen Watts Kearny, a career army officer who did not like Frémont, arrived in California that fall with 300 Dragoons, it put Frémont in a precarious position.

Had Frémont been trying to set up a government of his own, or had President Polk indeed sent him secret orders? The only two who could confirm the truth about Frémont and his actions were Lt. Gillespie, now dead, and the president himself. Polk wasn't denying or confirming anything about the incident. Frémont was, therefore, court-martialed and convicted of mutiny and disobedience for his troubles. He was pardoned from serving his sentence, but Frémont resigned his commission. The irony is that because of what happened to the man, he became that much more of a hero to the public, who largely viewed him as a martyr.

As the Mexican War came to an end, talk turned to the possibility of building a railroad to link the east coast to the west coast. Senator Benton persuaded a handful of St. Louis businessmen to finance an expedition through the Rocky Mountains to open a route that would take a transcontinental railroad from his native state of Missouri to San Francisco. He chose his son-in-law to lead the mission and Frémont eagerly accepted, wanting to redeem himself and once more become the hero of America.

Everything that had gone so well for Frémont on his first two expeditions west now went wrong. This expedition (1848–1849) turned into a disaster. He didn't have the benefit of Kit Carson for a guide this time out, although Old Bill Williams, the man he did choose for a guide, had been in the moun-

Senator Thomas Hart Benton,
Frémont's father-in-law

tains for more than forty years. But perhaps worst is the fact that Frémont began his expedition in late October ignoring Williams's advice that it was too late in the season to embark on such an escapade.

By mid-December, Old Bill Williams had led the party right into the San Juan Mountains where the temperature fell to 20° below zero and the snow was ten feet deep. When the trip was all over, Frémont would lay the blame on Williams, his guide. But, in retrospect, the expedition should never have started as late as it did. The cold and snow had numbed the sensibilities of everyone, and somewhere along the way Williams had turned the party north fifteen miles too soon. The weather only worsened as the team encountered a blinding snowstorm and their mules began to freeze to death. By then Frémont knew he had to turn back.

The day after Christmas, he sent Williams and three of his best men south to Taos for supplies. When Williams and his men hadn't returned sixteen days later, Frémont himself set out with a handful of men to find his guide. Slowly, the condition of his men worsened, and they began to drop by the side of the trail. When Frémont came on Williams and his men, he found that they, too, had run out of food and were near starvation.

With the help of some Ute Indians, Frémont

and his small band made it to a settlement. A rescue party returned for the remainder of the men in the stranded expedition. Frémont headed for Carson's home in Taos where, after receiving sufficient nourishment, he moved on alone to California, leaving what little was left of his party to shift for themselves. Eleven of the men in that party perished on the expedition.

In 1854, Frémont tried to penetrate the San Juan Mountain Range again. This expedition was just as disastrous. Yet, two years later, Frémont was still popular enough to become the first candidate to run for president on the newly founded Republican party ticket. He lost to James Buchanan, but his popularity among the people in the country continued to grow. The reports on his expeditions that he had submitted to Congress had been turned into pamphlets that would guide many a tenderfoot across the Oregon and California trails. The thousands of pioneers who would settle west of the Rockies were willing to overlook a few shortcomings in the life of a man who was largely responsible for getting them safely to their destination.

Because of that, John Charles Frémont would take a place in our history books as "the Great Pathfinder," even if he didn't quite live up to the name.

INDEX